DOING
— A LOT —
WITH A LITTLE

FEYI ABRAHAM ADESANYA

DOING A LOT WITH A LITTLE

COPYRIGHT ©2020
Feyi Abraham Adesanya

ISBN: 9798581419793

All rights reserved under international copyright law. Contents and/or cover may not be reproduced in any form without the express written consent of the author.

Unless otherwise indicated, all Scripture quotations are taken from the authorized King James Version of the Bible.

TABLE OF CONTENTS

Introduction	iv
Chapter 1 (ESTIMATE WHAT IT WILL TAKE)	1
Chapter 2 (WHAT DO YOU HAVE?)	4
Chapter 3 (APPRECIATE WHAT YOU HAVE)	8
Chapter 4 (KNOWLEDGE)	11
Chapter 5 (ORDER)	15
Chapter 6 (DISTRIBUTE)	20
Chapter 7 (GATHER UP THE FRAGMENTS)	25
Postscript	29

INTRODUCTION

From time to time, we will find ourselves in situations where what we have seem insufficient to meet the need at hand. There will always be such circumstances, it is not peculiar to the poor or needy, the rich too are faced with such circumstances albeit at a larger scale.

At that juncture where need overwhelms resources at hand, one is faced with two options- first, to resign to fate or the second, try to use what you have to get the job done. If you are the type of person who always goes for the first option you may never be able to do any notable thing. Big things always stretch us, they always do.

Introduction

Should you however go for the second option, I can assure you, you will be stretched, you may even falter on some instances, but you certainly will experience miracles- the miracle of doing a lot with a little.

The Bible records at least two separate instances where Jesus needed to feed a multitude of people but had only a few loaves and fishes. He too had the option of dodging the situation (in fact, his disciples advised him to so do) but he decided to take up the challenge and at the end of the day, five loaves and two fishes fed five thousand families and seven loaves and few little fishes fed four thousand (John 6:1-14, Mathew 15:32-38). Talk of doing a lot with a little, those are classic examples.

Introduction

We have long thought of these purely as miracles (and yes indeed they are) but looking closely at them, we find underlying principles Jesus employed to get the result. If we too employ those principles, we will end up with the same miracle of achieving great things with minimal resources. In the following chapters therefore, we shall understudy these principles.

ESTIMATE WHAT IT WILL TAKE

Chapter 1

Chapter 1

ESTIMATE WHAT IT WILL TAKE

Just as you can scarcely cure a disease you can't diagnose; you can't meet a need you can't describe nor can you find something you can 't recognize. The first step towards solving a problem that seems overwhelming or any problem at that is to first understand it. You have to be able to say clearly "this is the problem, and this is what I will need to solve it". To arrive at this, you will need to ask yourself frank questions and provide even franker answers.

Taking a cue from Jesus when He fed five thousand with five loaves and two fishes in John 6:1-14, in verse five, Jesus asked ***"…whence shall we buy bread, that these***

may eat? " to which Philip gave a rough estimate of two hundred pennies in verse seven. They realized they needed food, they counted the exact amount of people they needed to feed and they estimated how much that would cost them. Just that alone, puts them in a better place to solve the problem than somebody who just says "all I know is I have a multitude to feed"

Even when praying about a problem, you are likely to have your requests granted faster if it is precise hence you will find Jesus in the gospels asking people "what (exactly) do you want me to do for you?"

So, when you are faced with a huge task that your resources seem incapable of handling, first thing to do is estimate what exactly is needed, what it will take to solve it and possible ways of going about it.

WHAT DO YOU HAVE?

Chapter 2

Chapter 2

WHAT DO YOU HAVE?

I believe after Philip told Jesus two hundred penny worth of bread will scarcely be enough to feed the people, he would have expected Jesus to say something like "so where do we get more money?" but the account in Mark chapter six lets us know in verse thirty-eight that Jesus instead said to them **"How many loaves have ye? go and see".** This brings me to the second step to doing a lot with a little- Find out what you have.

Don't let what you need obscure what you have. No matter how humongous your need is, there is something you have with which you can solve the problem or at least begin to solve it. The solution is often in what you have, not what you don't have, look inward and around.

I imagine that the disciples must have reluctantly carried out the instruction of Jesus to go and see what they have in the camp, coming back with just a little child's meal must have been ridiculous but right there in that lunch box of five loaves and two fishes was more than enough food for the multitude. It is amazing that the solution was right there in the midst of the problem. It may not look like much, but there is always something you have with or around you that you can use to solve the problem. It could be time, it could be talent, it could be relationships, whatever it is, little as it may seem, it is useful.

Steve Harris' saying that "what limits you is not what you don't have but what you have but don't know how to use" is indeed very true. The widow of the late prophet in second Kings chapter four would have lost her children to slavery and died in excruciating poverty if not that Elisha's question about what she had pointed her to a bottle of oil she had always had. That next to nothing bottle of oil was her five loaves and two fishes with which she fed her multitude.

A few times, the solution will be some distance away, but most of the time, it is within and around. We must therefore train ourselves to take inventory of what we have.

APPRECIATE WHAT YOU HAVE

Chapter 3

Chapter 3

APPRECIATE WHAT YOU HAVE

Faced with a Goliath, the temptation will always be there to despise David, so you can't blame Andrew for remarking about five loaves and two fishes ***"...but what are they among so many" (John 6:9).*** You must however not fall for that temptation; you can't afford to despise your solution in its seed form otherwise you will be stranded.

Jesus took those loaves and in verse eleven of John chapter six, we are told He gave thanks and then began to distribute it.

Thanksgiving has multiplier effect; appreciation makes things appreciate. Instead of murmuring and complaining over the seeming little thing you have to handle that big task, if you are grateful and appreciate it, one way or the other, you will find that that little thing can actually do much. You will begin to get ideas and innovations that will help your David kill it's Goliath with just a sling.

As long as you keep focusing on the things you don't have which you think you need, you will find it hard to be grateful for what you have but if you abide by the philosophy that "what I have now is all I need now", you will be appreciative of what you have and consequently, what you have will appreciate to meet up with the demand.

KNOWLEDGE

Chapter 4

Chapter 4

KNOWLEDGE

"…He himself knew what he would do"- John 6:6

The difference between Jesus and His disciples at that instant when they needed to feed the multitude was simply this – Jesus knew what to do. What you know can make up for what you don't have, when you add great knowledge to little resources, it works like yeast and dough - little becomes much. Little resources plus knowledge of what to do with it will always do more than a combo of great resources and ignorance can do.

Knowledge is a multiplier; the more knowledgeable you are about a mater, the more you are able to do with little resources.

Knowledge

This is why you will find that some people are able to do so much with meager resources than what their contemporary are able to do with far more resources. Just throwing money at a problem usually doesn't solve the problem, you have to be well informed about the problem enough to dispense scarce resources wisely and accurately. Financial intelligence is more important than money.

This is not just true for money but for every kind of resource. I remember watching a Hollywood action movie some years ago, there was this scene where an FBI agent was caught unarmed by a gun wielding criminal. Seeing the size of the gun and the desperation of this criminal, I concluded the FBI agent had no chance of survival, not when he didn't even have a pen knife not to talk of a gun. He ran and dodged everywhere in the room as this other guy was shooting at him. I noticed though, that he was counting something, I wouldn't know what exactly it was that he was counting. Then all of a sudden, he stopped running away and started running towards the other guy who was shooting him and with his bare hands killed him.

He explained later that he by the sound of the gun knew the exact number of bullets in its cartridge, that was what he was counting. The moment the last bullet was out, he knew that guy would have to change cartridge which would give him a few seconds to get him. That was how a man with bare hands killed a man with a gun. The man without the gun was knowledgeable and that made up for the absence of a gun. Now imagine what he would do if he had a gun. Knowledge is very important in maximizing resources.

ORDER

Chapter 5

Chapter 5

ORDER

"and Jesus said, make the men sit down"- John 6:10

"And he said to his disciples, Make them sit down by fifties in a company." – Luke 9:14

You may wonder why Jesus asked that the people not only be seated but arranged into groups of fifties. He was putting order in place. Nothing will ever be enough where things are in disarray. Had He not arranged them, first, they won't be able to count and know exactly how many people that were there but arranged in groups of fifties, the counting and even the distribution becomes easy. Secondly, if Jesus hadn't arranged the multitude, there would have been uproar in

Order

the distribution of the bread. It is important to note that the bread was not multiplied until order was in place. Perhaps the multiplication of resources you seek is waiting for you to put order in place.

Order helps you maximize resources, time and energy. Disorderliness on the other hand is a waster of resources, time and energy. You must have noticed how little a bag can contain if you just dump in it the things you want to put in it as compared to how much more it can accommodate if you take the time to arrange the things inside it. It's as simple as that, you either take the pain of putting things in order or suffer insufficiency.

The more orderly you are with your finances, the more you will be able to do with little funds. The more orderly you are with your time, the more you will be able to get out of your time. Same for every resource. You will be surprised the multiplier effect structures and systems have on limited resources. Where there are no proper structures and systems in place that ensure orderliness, a lot of resources get wasted or stolen, Nigeria is a testament to that.

This is true for even spiritual resources. Without order, no matter the amount of anointing, little or nothing will be achieved, hence 1 Corinthians 14:40 says **"Let all things be done decently and in order."**

Small organizations often think this is something to do when you become big but the truth is that it is what you do to become big. So, if you are going to do a lot with as little as possible, you must be a suckler for

Order

order, you must put in place systems and structures.

DISTRIBUTE

Chapter 6

Chapter 6

DISTRIBUTE

"And Jesus took the loaves; and when he had given thanks, he distributed to the disciples, and the disciples to them that were set down; and likewise of the fishes as much as they would."- John 6:11

Did you notice that Jesus didn't distribute the bread straight to the multitude? He distributed it to the disciples who in turn distributed to the people. Two things to learn from this with respect to doing a lot with a little: First, when what you have is small compared to what you need, break down the task into bits and tackle it accordingly. There is a saying that there is only one way to eat an elephant - a bite at a time. No matter how big a problem is, the moment you can break it down, you have demystified it. That's what Jesus did; He didn't attempt to distribute the bread to all 5,000 plus people at once (that would be overwhelming), he shared it first among his disciples (a group of twelve) who in turn shared it among groups of fifties and as they did, the bread was miraculously multiplying. So, for instance, you have a massive vision but you don't have the kind of resources to pull it off yet. Rather than getting overwhelmed, break down that vision into small components that your present resources can handle, go for one component and as God multiplies you, move to another, before you know it you would be eating the last bit of the elephant.

The second thing here is that Jesus shared the bread first with His disciples - a group of people who not only love Him but believed in Him, He leveraged on His relationship with them. If you are going to maximize your resources, you need people, you need quality relationships. What you lack in resources, you can make up for with relationships.

Distribute

In fact, people can open their resources up to you on the strength of your relationship with them. The less quality relationships you have, the more resources you will need to get things done. You just can't do much without the help and input of others. If Jesus needed people, you certainly will need too so don't trivialize relationships.

Men are God's best method of intervening in our affairs. A miracle can be stalled if you don't have quality relationship with people around you, a case in point is the story of the prophet's widow in 2 Kings 4:1-7, God was going to miraculously multiply the oil but the multiplication was dependent on the amount of vessels she was able to borrow from her neighbors which of course was dependent on her relationship with them. In the end, her little oil turned to the much it did and stopped multiplying not when the power of God stopped but when she maxed out on her relationships.

Do you have a huge task to undertake with little resources? Share the burden with a few people close to you first, their buy-in will help you a great deal. They will often be the ones who will help you reach the multitude you want to reach. Most small businesses and even ministries that have become big had their friends and families as their first
and for some time their only customers, audience and partners. It was these "disciples" who then brought onboard others. That's how things often multiply - organically.

GATHER UP THE FRAGMENTS

Chapter 7

Chapter 7

GATHER UP THE FRAGMENTS

"When they were filled, he said unto his disciples, Gather up the fragments that remain, that nothing be lost."- John 6:12

To maximize resources, you have got to first block every leakage- that is, stop everything hemorrhaging your resources. Even if you have a lot, it still makes sense not to waste not to talk of when you don't have enough. Everything has to be accounted for. Waste hinders divine provision. God hates waste and so when He sees that the resources He has provided is not well managed, He stops the flow. He is magnanimous but not prodigal.

Gather up the fragments

Not only do you have to block leakages of your resources, you must also become a recycler- you gather every remainder and find use for it, that way you will be able to milk out completely everything there is in the resources at your disposal. That's what Jesus did by asking that the remaining bread be gathered and guess what, they had 12 baskets left. My guess is that they sold them and the money was put in the purse of the ministry. You'll be shocked how much value there is in what people call left over.

Poor people often term the rich who insist on "gathering up the fragment" as being stingy, but no they are not, they are just being frugal and frugality is a virtue not a vice. Often times, the defining factor between the rich and the poor is not the difference in income but the ability to manage waste. If you can't gather up the fragment, no matter how much you have, you will end up with nothing.

Postscript

CHOOSING TO FOLLOW JESUS

It will be robbery to have shared with you in this book all that I have shared and not give you an opportunity to accept Jesus into your life.

Jesus died to save us all from our sins and from everlasting damnation; He came to make us children of God. Anyone who dies without receiving Jesus is damned forever; you must not let that happen to you. I challenge you today, if you have not done it before, to accept to follow and live for Jesus from today.

If you want to accept Him into your life, from your heart say this simple prayer:

"Jesus, I acknowledge that I am a sinner and helpless without you. Today, I accept you as my saviour from sin. Forgive me of every sin I have ever committed and please cleanse me from every form of defilement. Come and take your place in my life and make me yours. Thank you for hearing me. Amen"

It may even be that you just need to rededicate your life to Him; If that is the case, just ask Him to forgive you and take you back. You may say the prayer above as a re-affirmation of your faith. Find a bible-believing church within your neighbourhood and begin to fellowship with them,

Postscript

they will explain the way of the Lord more to you and help you grow in your new-found faith.

God bless You!

LET'S CONNECT

Feyi Abraham Adesanya, The Teacher Ministries

@FeyiAdesanya

@feyi_abraham_adesanya

The Teacher Ministries

feyiabrahamadesanya@gmail.com, theteacherministries@gmail.com

www.theteacherministries.wordpress.com

NOTES

NOTES

ABOUT THE BOOK

From time to time, we are faced with situations where what we have is little compared to what we believe we need. This is a situation not peculiar to the poor, even the rich experience it. Maximizing resources is therefore a much needed skill. Gleaning from how Jesus multiplied bread and fish to feed the multitude, this book will put in your hands, time tested principles that will help you multiply and maximize the resources at your disposal.

ABOUT THE AUTHOR

Feyi Abraham Adesanya is a lover of God's word and a sound teacher of the same. His simple, humorous and powerful presentation of the word of God endears him to his many listeners around the globe. Among other things, he is passionate about helping youths discover and fulfill God's purpose for their lives.

He is founder and president of The Teacher Ministries, a non-denominational platform committed to teaching the truth of the word of God emphasizing its integrity and power. He is married to Olabisi Adesanya and blessed with two beautiful children.

www.ingramcontent.com/pod-product-compliance
Lightning Source LLC
Chambersburg PA
CBHW072238230526
45466CB00025B/2114